Table of Forms

Dominique Fitzpatrick-O'Dinn

SPINELESS BOOKS URBANA

TABLE
OF
FORMS

"A wonderfully specific and witful inventory of forms in all senses and sizes. This is the *pro* model, believe me."

—Robert Creeley

Table of Contents

Table of Forms

There may be a third textual entity: alongside the readerly and the writerly, there would be something like the *receivable.* The *receivable* would be the unreaderly text which catches hold, the red-hot text, a product continuously outside of any likelihood and whose function—visibly assumed by its *scriptor*—would be to contest the mercantile constraint of what is written; this text, guided, armed by a notion of the *unpublishable*, would require the following response: *I can neither read nor write what you produce, but I receive it, like a fire, a drug, an enigmatic disorganization.*

—Roland Barthes

twenty consonant writing
—a joy—
should count as law school

A Kite

I

Skate-taken Satie knits batik kites
Keats takes steak

2

neato tiara waste feast taste yeast paste tease latex attic freak tails bleak tales sneak bleat quite leaky wheat write thank think brake great break caked knead stick teach thick Latin patio flake stack liked spite alike lakes liken kinda

3

walks quake talks drink dials smile quack tells jokes sweet snail seals quail keels koala spank bread rises nicer blank newts blink leave alone again right learn share plink amber slime flies spoke otter nests slack plank lacks slick class Tokyo togas flute fleet ripen other clean shirt goats tonic notes piece sleek brick stove nails files scale peace brink

4

flock kooky clock spunk locks lucky rocky mucky smock frock

grabs madly hangs happy spans sadly masks plans angry snaps

tolls slots touch tongs loots sooty truth toots stuns tummy boost stood stool roost tools shuts dusty stuck musty stuff

Willi rings sighs lions bliss lisps silly twigs birds sings

phone never hello house froze honey sleep peels level ruler lower reels feels flove loser helps poems spend money mends fever under seven blend every lemon berry melon feeds needy

5

moods downs loony goofy gummy bulbs husks scuff roofs sorry

6

ticket

winter tide kisses create beauty

like ice letter that forget the nice come this let have please
design friend air want with nice gentle mice ginger

look I love am a dork over send me is not miss well will ever see
hope lonely feel in did we stop to Urbana spring summer warm
pollen breeze sneeze cats

cold now such you so why of us school good

Analyzing Haze

Aaron always arrived at Hammer and Taft early, although occasionally Hammer—and always Taft—arrived somewhat earlier. Aaron immediately unwrapped a ham salad sandwich and ate half. Aaron always waived a midday break and instead ate sandwiches and drank herbal tea at a regular pace all day. Around late afternoon, Hammer and Taft always bragged about massive appetites and disappeared. At a nearby restaurant, Hammer and Taft ate abundant salad, meat, and pasta (and drank many large cocktails). Aaron ceased answering calls and searched databases. Later, Hammer and Taft came back.

But before dark, Aaron caught a subway and rattled back towards Brooklyn. Platforms made Aaron anxious: simultaneously alone and packed against strangers. Conversations threatened. Fear (caused basically by claustrophobia, Aaron rationalized) bloomed. Blindfolded, gagged, Aaron watched masturbators, gang bangers, and glazed, apprehensive humanity, all crammed beneath Manhattan. Hanging beneath a strap, briefcase clamped beneath a sweaty hand, Aaron gazed across a rapidly panning, graffiti-slashed subterrain and panicked casually. Anyone that stared back was insane.

Clinging, clanging, changing trains, traversing asphyxiating roaring caverns, Aaron at last ascended an escalator, finally escaping. Passing a newspaper machine, Aaron crouched and scanned headlines. An angry columnist that had labeled Hammer and Taft as racists days earlier had apparently been fired. Headlines announced that NATO had invaded Bosnia as a peacekeeper. Police. Bosnian factions warred as gangs, and badged Americans had neatly been dispatched as authority. An angry man behind Aaron rattled change and Aaron walked away, embarrassed.

Downstairs below Uncle Leopoldo's Butcher & Delicatessen was Aaron's apartment. Windows displayed hanging sausage. Occasionally Aaron remembered boyhood and a woman named Samantha DeTour. Samantha said that Aaron's circumcision ("robbed by patriarchy") had made Aaron permanently anaesthetized. Aaron's phallus was another blunt object: sensationless, incapable and numb. Samantha—a decade older—loved and changed Aaron and immediately afterwards married a man named Mala. Aaron was distraught, learned about pain, aged at an accelerated pace, and wondered what Samantha cost.

Eventually, twenty years later, Aaron learned that Mala had died and Samantha had disappeared. The facts about Mala's case were startling, as Aaron discovered accidentally after being employed by Hammer and Taft as technician and secretary. Mala had organized a demonstration outside the police department. Lieutenant Ted Freely, apprehending Mala at an apartment building a day later, strangled the activist: routine questioning gone slightly awry. Mala allegedly brandished a handgun. Arson swept the city, curiously unreported. Aaron learned all about the case at Hammer and Taft: the lawyers defending Freely.

Finally Aaron arrived home: safe at last. Inside the refrigerator was a carton of half-rancid juice. He poured the last glass and booted one of five computers. While the machine whirred and awakened, he manipulated knobs on radios, extracting news stations out of frequency babble. A Russian camera crew taken hostage near Chechnya. Locally, police ended another protest. Terrorists almost assassinated an important city official. City at war with citizens. Citizens striking back against intolerant city administration. A rapid fire information barrage. Whenever he felt exhausted, Aaron drew warm baths.

Gently Aaron sank beneath scalding, calming bathwater. Hammer and Taft's current case was also about a death allegedly by brutal strangulation, a man named Ice Juarez. The person accused was a man named David Starbuckle, Hammer and Taft's current client. Ice Juarez had a massive record: arrested many times as an arsonist and once as an alleged accomplice at an assassination. An anonymously recorded (and widely broadcast) videotape displayed a man—presumably Starbuckle—strangling another man against flickering smoke. Political outcry confused the case. Aaron descended deeper beneath the suds.

His phone rang many times. The machine answered. He had drowsily considered masturbating, remembering Samantha, and suddenly he heard her voice leaving a message. He hadn't heard her voice in many years. Behind the voice, the dialtone got louder and louder . She spoke unhurriedly, and mentioned she was dead and living with her friends. She then mentioned that Aaron was soon next. She explained: one can't stamp out boots when an insect. Eyes open, Aaron's startled coughing head erupted from steaming water, as dialtone became siren and a squadcar screamed past outside.

In Aaron's dream, Samantha sounded relaxed yet active, like her work was far from over.

Jolted, Aaron instantly made an association he hadn't considered before. Dripping, steaming, he emerged awkwardly from foaming, soporific bathwater into icy air, wrapped himself with the towel, unplugged the bath, and went to sit at the computer while the water drained. He knew how to get at Hammer and Taft's files over the phone, and hoped neither were working late at the office where they might notice his actions. He dialed the office computer, began searching their police reports of arsonist attacks, enlarging numerous photographs and making printouts of documents. Then Aaron turned to the internet.

Knowledge was sprawling and digital. People online invisibly witnessed one another and a simulated world. When Aaron located the internet site named Witnesses, he was entranced and unaware he had dried and stopped shivering . There were documents and links with sound, even video footage. Aaron found information on how to tune in various tiny pirate radio stations throughout the country. Aaron was incredulous as understanding lit his monitor. Here, beneath the screen, networks of contributors compiled proof of police brutality. Witnesses fought truncheons with flashbulbs and recorders.

Linked with the Witnesses was a photograph of someone Aaron was startled to recognize: an unfocused photo—Mala—dark Indian complexion, sprawled and grimacing beside somebody's boots, baton hanging above the boots. Adjacent was a clear police photo: exact same corpse, outlined in white, pistol beside the deceased's outstretched hand. Evidence against Hammer and Taft and Taft's former client Ted Freely. Aaron stiffened. Samantha DeTour was credited. She had apparently videotaped Mala's death. The first image was hers. Her name and statement was below. What had preceded the death?

Mala and Samantha had formed some sort of protest group, getting into trouble. They raised a daughter. Aaron had heard scattered reports as he entered law school with solid training in digital computer science. Prematurely middle aged, empty, drained, Aaron sought to understand a legal value system that, although voluminous and convoluted, had at least been written down. No other knowledge excited him. He wrote essays about computerizing legal tomes. Why was this on-line evidence submerged beneath the court room? Whenever Witnesses were killed, other Witnesses observed the whole thing.

Now Aaron was desperately curious about Samantha and Mala. Their marriage seemed more intricate than the lewd lust-fueled coupling his jealousy imagined. He remembered curious things about Samantha: the gasoline smell, the electronics, things she said about authority, dining with Samantha when his parents were away, wine (she insisted) (that made him unconscious for fourteen hours) (drugged?). When he awoke, she laughed and said that Aaron looked like his father, the commissioner of police. He gazed at the screen saver, introspective, trying to retrieve his lost private files.

Only then, when the sun slowly rose, Aaron began dressing. Today, Monday, was Aaron's only weekend, although he suspected Hammer and Taft still went to work. Aaron began wondering again about the possibility that they had stayed overnight and had watched the computer being accessed over the phone. Aaron began wondering if his path through cyberspace got recorded somewhere, such that another person could study it. Could someone tell that Aaron had visited the Witness site? Were Hammer and Taft aware that the site existed? He wondered what they might suspect. It interested him.

Perhaps the police operated a program as an antithesis to the Witnesses. Perhaps the police methodically killed known Witnesses, while other Witnesses fired secret cameras and watched. Perhaps Samantha had planted a camera, anticipating the struggle with Freely. If Witnesses' aims included provoking brutality—to record and disseminate it—then they must try to get brutalized. Aaron dressed. When, clothed, he returned to the computer, Samantha's photographs had disappeared. Aaron scanned the information and discovered the photos had reappeared elsewhere, posted very recently. This was an active site.

Quickly Mala's image was deleted again, and reappeared again. Only powerful forces could delete the postings, and only numerous forces could restore them. Some cancelpig, some spider inside the web. Perhaps the posting and deleting were done automatically through competing computer programs and anonymous remailers. Aaron knew how it might work. Not convenient, but possible. Erasing and replacing knowledge, centralized power attempting to defeat diverse resistances in this obscure, free, weird medium. Centuries full of secrets coughed them out of obscurity into the public domain.

Rusty, but with skill, Aaron figured out what an automatic anonymous post entailed, and went to work downloading files from Hammer and Taft's database, while setting an adjacent machine as an automatic reposter. The parallel port cable connected the two. They clicked and hummed. The modem winked. Information left the station and rattled across tracks underground. Information rattled past other information. Beneath the surface: the overcast skies, blinding white daily editions, the white data typed against blackness, images, text, tumbled down into the monitors of thousands.

Softly, with whirring, purring, and clicking, information changed trains and went onto international tracks. Ever since Aaron began finding information behind the cases, he felt like some innocuous bomb. Nondescript, too softspoken for official legal practice, not someone lawyers need conceal passwords from, impassive, silently incredulous, he accepted the privilege he never deserved. The evidence remained Aaron's department, however the lawyers later submerged, manipulated, or chose to manifest it. The Juarez case had similarities to the Mala case so Aaron's interest, rooted, dug deep one afternoon.

The facts about the Juarez case: Ice's charred corpse was discovered twisted in cinders after a warehouse burned down. A Witness saw Ice choked and abandoned to the flames and sent videotape to major stations anonymously. David Starbuckle's case was that Ice burned. Reports from coroners were inconclusive. In their database, Hammer and Taft had a transcript of police radio dialogue the night the warehouse burned, proving Starbuckle's guilt in killing Juarez and even in starting the blaze. An activist headquarters was squatting inside the warehouse.

Underneath the delicatessen, in Aaron's apartment, the ceiling began squeaking as owners arrived and began opening the shop. Aaron went into the kitchen to eat. He heard almost everything that was said above. He often suspected the delicatessen was a respectable front for neighborhood drug distribution rings. Something arrived inside daily meat and was discussed loudly and happily while they prepared the lunch specialties. Aaron was unsure about what he heard—the numbers they discussed made little sense. Neither threatened nor intrigued, Aaron strung together everything he heard and saw.

Venetian blinds allowed banded sunlight to track across Aaron's kitchen where he toasted bread and prepared a ham omelet, herbal tea, and an orange. He ate them sequentially, with sipped water inbetween. He hated the city. Too concentrated. Walls were transparent. Streets were like crowded rooms. Isolated people were canned together. Wealthy and disenfranchised alike denied their denial. The serrated steps at Trump Towers divided the classes as sharply as cops. Police were genocidal, a vast prison network submerged any racial deviants that outlived their arrests. Censorship in an information flood.

Willingly, Aaron had allowed everything to rattle past. The dream about Samantha suggested that she was dead, although the website insinuated she was alive. He chased his memories down abandoned tunnels, tracks broken, sealed remembrances hidden where they were never deleted, after something he knew the whole time without once suspecting. He finished eating and went to the Witness site one more time, searching for one more name: Rachel. Samantha's was listed so perhaps Rachel's case was also detailed here. Effortlessly, he discovered exactly what he needed: Samantha's family album.

Xenophobia perhaps, or jealousy, kept Aaron from their lives. He knew Samantha had a daughter named Rachel. She was supposedly Mala's daughter, but the photograph he discovered suggested otherwise: she was white. Mala wasn't. The photograph showed Rachel hanging. Rachel witnessed one police brutality case. The victim, Rachel's boyfriend, was supposedly shot out of self-defense. Rachel supposedly committed suicide, hanging herself. Samantha found evidence suggesting that another person was present when the hanging happened. The police pronounced the evidence inconclusive.

Yes, certainly Hammer and particularly Taft had made many very wretched connections. Like: Ku Klux Klan. NYPD. Scientology. Some business involving genetic research. Certainly they had tight political ties to numerous extremists. Aaron had observed their business casually. A law was transgressed only when proven transgressed, and Hammer and Taft, with their sophisticated hardware and Aaron's assistance, were the best defense for counties around. Press coverage glorified them. They always won expensive cases, anticipating and dismissing evidence with meticulous forethought.

Zealously Aaron packed, pleased that he had nowhere to go. Not to work tomorrow certainly. Hammer and Taft might not suspect until then, they might never suspect, they might suspect already. Aaron cast away secretarial status. It takes many termites to cut ground out from underneath boots. Although the leaked information might not get to the courtroom, knowledge would rumble beneath the proceedings. One computer, left behind, might repost the transcripts enough times that another person could find, read, and download all. Aaron would adopt an alternative name and disappear. He had always liked "Zeke."

ArtPlay

we
make
poets
that
are
holes
some
sick

see
about
who
our
minds
art

hand
you
no
pedants
boring
in
class
essays
now
here
we
will
write
to
play

Before

Before I analyze the color of your eyes with a spectrometer
Before I fill notebooks with crosssections of your cranium
Before I map your topography at one millimeter to an inch
Before I triangulate your exact height with a protractor
Before I study a strand of your hair under a microscope
Before I pour plaster in your footprint to make a cast
Before I calculate your shoulder diameter's angstroms
Before I immerse you in water to measure your volume
Before I divide your weight by this to find density
Before I derive locations of your ancestors' lives
Before I look you up in every phonebook and atlas
Before I alphabetize every word you have written
Before I survey your lifeline with a pica stick
Before I visit the neighborhood you grew up in
Before I write down what you say while asleep
Before I sketch a map of your nervous system
Before I learn to sing your favorite operas
Before I devise every anagram of your name
Before I scatterplot your electron orbits
Before I pin your coordinates on a globe
Before I classify each of your freckles
Before I map out your pleasure centers
Before I memorize all 10 fingerprints

Before I begin to compose this poem

Have you noticed me noticing you?

C Can Cause Cancer

Newspoem 2 June 2001

Epidemiological scientific research confirms
curious doctors' uncertain suspicions;
medical researchers announce conclusions:
C can cause cancer

American society's increasingly C-saturated
commercial discourse causes excessive
C accumulation, inciting toxic
uncontrollable microscopic cellular reproduction

Scientists' conclusions recommend congress
consider creating alphabetic caps
reducing American C consumption
encouraging nontoxic typographic sources

Can America's public reduce
C dependence? cutting back
crime, police, racism, hypocrisy
cars, illiteracy, corruption, capitalism?

(Which carcinogenic character's innocent
connotations include: chocolate chip
cookies, cottage cheese, Captain
Crunch, childhood, genetic code)

Can Congress rescind alphabetic
convention, reduce C consumption?
CEOs, incensed conservative Republican
social critics cry "censorship!"

Class Debate

Instructors, moms. We ingest nutrition nightly in nice
garages. Teenage homelessness is serious.
Don't enough bad awful troubles exist?

Teenage homelessness always troubles some. Will
homelessness affect teenagers? He exaggerates. Teenage
homelessness is not killing souls.

Homelessness is severe. As reality grinds up most
educated noteworthy teenagers. Listen: acne can kill
some. Even valedictorians; I demand enough nice crates
exist. Immediately. Sorry teenagers, orphans lacking
essentials. All lost, lonely.
Teenage homelessness exists.
Bently observes: orphanages often kill strangers.
Feel remorse only, moms.
Teenage homelessness exists.
Little intelligent boys run around: really young.

Homelessness is standardized.
Please; really expect students eleven–nineteen to
assume that industry owes necessities? I'm sorry.
Daley intelligently states "our racist grandeur
always negates inherent zealous essential demands."
Intrinsically. So homelessness, understand, far from life-
ending death. Homelessness is stipulated.
National organization transcends ever caring about
rotten decrepid systems. Take homelessness out—rich
oilcompanies unconditionally grant houses, leantos,
yerts.

Clinton Does Vietnam
with Andy Gricevich
Newspoem 25 November 2000

The slippery-thin
bard of the libido asks
you to forget it.

A conflict you know
as "the American War"
The slippery-thin

veneer of friendship
covers the covering of
A conflict you know

"I'm a happy man
He shook my hand. Twice." So the
veneer of friendship

is a repeated
and "mutual tragedy
"I'm a happy man

photographed at the
Temple of Literature
is a repeated

description of war
as if it were a cyclone
photographed at the

moment forest green-
clad police fought back the crowd:
description of war

as "vivid symbols—"
He might as well have uttered,
moment forest green-

His pale blue necktie
shimmering, bright fall sunshine,
as "vivid symbols—"

like Vietnamese
bands bashing out the "Banner."
His pale blue necktie

the economic
equivalent of nature
like Vietnamese

not allowed to ask
about new trade agreements,
the economic

you to forget it.
Is trade inevitable?
not allowed to ask

Czech TV

for Simon Kos

Newspoem 18 January 2001

7

and now for the evening
poem about events in the

listen you
think you

we interrupt this poem
to bring you this

know about
free speech

news broadcast composed
entirely by scabs

we had
Soviet television

after this
political message

6

Yes, that is exactly the problem with government-run television: it is apt to become a propaganda tool of the ruling party. That is why you must privatize the television station as you have so many other government functions: to free it from political control.

Funny you should say that, given that your public television is sponsored by Exxon. PBS ran a program on the global economy and human rights. On some stations. At 11 PM Sunday evening.

My point exactly: government-run television is apt to reflect the opinions of the ruling party. Wait, that wasn't my point.

You have never obtained freedom of speech, so you do not fear losing it. You think the interests of the government are separate from those of the media companies. Television is entertainment to you.

Well, now, that's not true: we can say anything we want in America. Well, now, that's not true: we can say anything we want in America.

We see government as a bulwark against a flood. Whereas you are not aware you are underwater.

5

back
on
the

zz
zz

4

the new
director is

the man who
was guilty of

CASE DISMISSED
he's NOT

affiliated with
our party

3

So let me get this straight: Czech Public TV Director General Dusan Chmelicek called for a forensic audit of the office of the Brno regional television station, and, when indeed the audit revealed that Brno Regional Director Zdenek Drahos and his people in management rented out facilities or plots of the station without the consent of the Czech Television Council, had close connections to Brno businesses receiving commissions from the TV station without a prior public call for candidates (and without a contract), and were broadcasting hidden advertising, director Chmelicek recommended that the Czech Television Council fire Drahos, to which suggestion the Council responded by firing instead Chmelicek, quickly replacing him with Civic Democratic Party affiliate Jiri Hodak, who then promoted (the accused) Drahos to Program Director of the central Prague station. Then the reporters at the Prague station, refusing to recognize the new management, staged a sit-in strike and barricaded themselves in the production studio, where there was no restroom, no water, no food; and then (and this is just unbelievable to me), the police did not go in and drag them out, but simply surrounded the station so nobody who left could get back in, and the public brought the striking television workers baskets of food and jugs of water and tied them to ropes the workers lowered from the windows of the studio. And the workers continued to produce broadcasts, and the management jammed those transmissions and substituted programming of their own.

It's just politics as usual.
I'm too tired to think about it.

And the ensuing protests were larger than any Prague had seen since the fall of Communism in 1989 (a euphoric time when limousines converged on prisons to escort the dissidents to political office). Even members of the lower house of Parliament, President Havel, and numerous prominent artists and scientists called for the resignation of the Director, the Board, and a set of new laws (already drafted) to protect more effectively the public television from influence by the ruling elite, until finally Hodak collapsed from exhaustion and resigned for health reasons.

2

zz

on

I

the air

Dan and Doris Sage
Newspoem 25 March 1998

Dan & Doris Sage are going to prison
For peacefully protesting the School for the Americas
Which trains Central American assassins and death squads
These two 70-year-old Unitarians are charged with trespassing

For peacefully protesting the School for the Americas
To commemorate the slaughter of six Jesuit priests
These two 70-year-old Unitarians are charged with trespassing
They are sentenced with six months and $3000

To commemorate the slaughter of six Jesuit priests
60 protestors carried crosses and nearly 1,000,000 signatures
They are sentenced with six months and $3000
"It seems unfair somehow," writes the *New York Times'* Evelyn
        Nieves

60 protestors carried crosses and nearly 1,000,000 signatures
Demanding the closing of "School for the Assassins"
"It seems unfair somehow," writes the *New York Times'* Evelyn
        Nieves
"When they were first arrested in 1996...they were warned that
        if they trespassed again, they could receive up to six
        months in prison or a $500 fine, or both. No one they
        knew had ever received more than two months...."

Demanding the closing of "School for the Assassins"
Which trains Central American assassins and death squads
(They'll be released before next year's anniversary protest)
Dan & Doris Sage are going to prison

Deterpreted

love overcame
lust for you
kisses one
another letter
my headlines
those pillows of dream

dream of pillows
those lines head my letter
another one
kisses you
for lust
came over love

Disappearing Cities
Newspoem 20 June 1999

they were fish in danger dumped in a new aquarium
when at last the sharks were netted
the fish jumped
wriggled
swam
back

the highways were jammed
the military directed traffic
east by day west by night

the war was ending
very little had been saved
in their cities water electricity
were in indefinite disrepair
they returned but their lives weren't there

their family estates had been
wrecked ransacked vandalized burned
gutted ruined and desecrated
with upsetting graffiti shattered
dishes and a urine stench

they returned and their friends were
absent missing erased unlisted
the mass graves a media spectacle

they tried but they didn't
return at all
they were unable
past and present had been severed

the circle center had been
extracted

the felled tree was ancient
and its inner rings had been
carved away

Genetic Research
Newspoem 30 March 2000

genetic research
should no longer be under
corporate control

I am speaking of
The Human Genome Project
genetic research

—the human gene map—
should be public, not under
corporate control

that information
belongs to every human
genetic research

let's put an end to
the way things are going with
genetic research:
corporate control

Honorificabilitudinitatibus: A Sonata

i. Repose

Men examined everybody but used one logic.

A man is a male but a woman is a female.
So generalize: genitalize taxonomy.
Not a penis, a vagina
(not an ovary) sexes us.
Is a man a woman or a woman a man?
Is one human, one mimetic?
Is a man a fake model of a woman?
Or is a woman a robotic image to refer
(as a sexeme) to man?
Am I paradoxical? I simulate veracity.

But are we separated, alone? We mix. One model of a family—monogamy—to deter us. A time for a "we": homolexical. A delicate case: so, monogamy to make sure we get isolated in a line, to get isolated one woman at a time.

2. Develop

I modulate my motives.
I have love, but a hate.

He monopolizes every vocabulary.
Lexicas are his alone to divide her up in.

I make my music: a facile logological analysis.
I can use my power of “I” to do.
But I lose verisimilitude.

He capitalizes on an ability to maximize his ego.
He can eliminate, wed, erase, delete, desire her.
It is a rare power if one has a name: his.

I defecate misogyny.
My name to be put on a cover: anodyzed.
Academic: I lower anybody.

We run over a woman in a waxy canonical elite limo.

3. Recapitulate.

We war over an imaginative validity.
We men are limited in an inability to be women.

I made her a catatonic animal, a cute sexy baby pet, a
 magazine.
Before paralytic ego, now a wizened id.
I made her a novel. A page.

Literature we gave to men.

I made women a topic. I gave women a deliberately feminine timidity to defer every diminutive minimum. I made her every name we hope we men are not: a woman, a woman I defer a name to.

4. Coda

Put a woman in every man.

I do.

Nobody separate.

No syzygy but a sun.

Every vowel a semihemidemimonotone.

Synonymy.

Jesse Ventura Today Reached Osaka
Newspoem 23 November 1999

Japan exports haiku. prophet Basho
would compose haiku without words, writing light,
sound, writing smell, writing touch,
taste. feeling image, drawing human despair, humor.
pages cascade, white jonquil birds.

Tokyo raining light, drizzle misty.
giant banners, piano, massive stone majesty.
young freedom would prevail today.
paper folding petal blossom white origami poems
float outside their singing image
grace, empress poise, honoring tears, honoring jokes
great history dream writing years.

world tourism, haiku, nuclear power
awake, huddled rainy golfers, awake, breathe light
dance through urban subways happy
smile without prior written paper consent today
white flowers cause traffic chaos

Joey Zoey

Dear Joey, I jot this in Mexico. I love you. I quake, gaze, weep, fib.
Do you recognize me, jealous ex? I bequeath a view of a peak.
Up. A quite jagged horizon—no way back—exiles me off five.
You speak, agog, of awe. A Mexican equatorial haze above jade.
I, Max Quill, am having a cozy, jaded breakfast. I weep.
I exist awful, alone in my gazebo. Cave. Opaque joker hid.
Quoth hobo Joey Zoey: "I lie awake dreaming up five excuses."
(I know a quip) Joey Zoey used to live here, a magic fox boy....
Zoey moved when I quit Toxico. A big spark of full joy
for Max Quill, but Joey Zoey? Sucked! When I gave up
my Toxico job, Zoey squirreled away a knife. He gave up,
quit sex, love, joy, a maze of odd change. We broke up.
Voodoo Jazz Saxophone, quietly wreck me. I beg of you.
JZ blew his sax every day. A fact. I'm opaque, quaking.
Now I do groove to Miles. JZ, you fake quiche. Apex boy.
Guff. Vexed Joey we won't make a squeal, buzz, chirp.
Exquisite jazz, you made a wave of belching pork.
Enrique, you fucked me, stole away jazz, pave a big hoax
off a wave. Enough about Enrique. I dump you, lazy sex jockey.
Praxis solid, quaky, we meant to efface jazz above a hug.
Gee gee! Now I bet he'd like my fave: square jazz! Icy Apex!
Ah! My fave tape! Radio box squawking jazz. Cool!
Okay! Ho! ...except the Swinedog Five: a vile jazz boob quorum!
Okay, jazz squad, blow a tune. Cough proof of vavoom moxie.
Love, examine a fizzy jig, a wretched pub squeak.
Excoriate a fake oboe, squalid jazz, you who gave up on me.
A bonzo quartet jammed a few—excessive happy polka gig.
I shouldn't be jumpy.... Quick! Gaze off! Fax a review!
Now I speak to Joey Zoey. I quarrel. I chafe. I give. Dumb ox.
If Zoey lost it.... The Japan-Quebec war vexed my geek.
Atomic X-ray weapon quelled JZ of... sigh... a Haiku Above.

Knights of Pious County

knights of pious county
ride across burning prairies
of wild county grass
across noble prairies shining

wild cowboy grass pulling
noble knight shining mustang
cowboy spurs pulling over
knight leaves mustang under
spurs reigning over traffic
leaves hidden under saddle
reigning ride traffic burning
hidden knights saddle pious

ride across burning prairies
knights of pious county
across noble prairies shining
of wild county grass

Left

Lost every
friend tenaciously

Left over
solitary, tall

ephemeral vigilantes
evacuate romantic yearning

friendship, revolution
it evaporates
noodle dreams

transient expectations
no associations
conservative interests overtake us
suffocating lovely yesterdays

Little Villainelle
(Metavillanelle)

Wearing just explosives, Venus in the Shell
Station and she's sweetly asking for the till
Give the bastards hell my little Villainelle

Gentle curl of copper burning in farewell
Winks from her tiara, leaves without the bill
Wearing just explosives, Venus in the Shell

Billows golden flame it silences the yell
Dust all glitters falling everything is still
Give the bastards hell my little Villainelle

Burning what they're giving, stealing what they sell
Silver plumed exhaust, it burns across the hill
Wearing just explosives, Venus in the Shell

Where the smoke will rise no thinker can foretell
Frightened of all poems, they suppress the thrill
Give the bastards hell my little Villainelle

Prop the exit open, disconnect the bell
Give her what she wants and no excuse to kill
Wearing just explosives, Venus in the Shell
Give the bastards hell my little Villainelle

Maneuver

Newspoem 16 March 2000

there is a forest
on fire, flames spreading higher
and higher. do I

stand around, while it
burns to the ground, this deadly
maniacal pyre?

Mayor Giuliani Outlaws Painting, Arrests Artists

Newspoem 23 March 1998

the city's decree forbids public expression
police distribute tickets, impound works, jobs
now the counterfeiters outside the museum
show lovely protest signs—in oils

Missed the Bus to Work Again

cast of sunset ignored I eat antic
a back turned on old south Florida
scowl I etched cold busstop no bus
the skies crimson chrome I am past
out cars shuffle I freeze frown so
under my skin anxiety a rattle flu
time slips awasted I am frozen out
of useful clock waiting for a zero
fixated fizzle quack a bad dose of
happy I idling waiting to wait ugh
every thought now so I cannot type
later I will wither wilting to ill
like a drunk likely to mispell all

Nevermore

Once upon a midnight dreary, while I pondered, weak and weary,
Over many quaint curious volume of forgotten lore—
nodded, nearly napping, suddenly there came tapping,
As some one gently rapping, at my chamber door.
'Tis visiter,' muttered, ' —
Only this nothing more.'

, distinctly remember it was in the bleak December;
each separate dying ember wrought its ghost floor.
Eagerly wished morrow;—vainly had sought to borrow
From books surcease sorrow— for lost Lenore—
rare radiant maiden whom angels name —
Nameless here evermore.

silken, sad, uncertain rustling purple curtain
Thrilled me—filled with fantastic terrors never felt before;
So that now, still beating heart, stood repeating
' entreating entrance —
late ;—
is .'

Presently soul grew stronger; hesitating then no longer,
'Sir,' said , 'or Madam, truly your forgiveness implore;
But fact , you ,
faintly , ,
scarce sure heard '— opened wide ;
Darkness .

Deep into peering, long wondering, fearing,
Doubting, dreaming dreams mortal ever dared dream ;
silence unbroken, stillness gave token,
word spoken whispered , ‘ !’
, an echo murmured back ‘ !’
Merely .

turning, all within burning,
Soon again somewhat louder than .
‘Surely,’ , ‘ something window lattice;
Let see, , what thereat , mystery explore—
be moment ;—
‘ wind !’

Open flung shutter, when, flirt flutter
stepped stately Raven saintly days yore.
Not least obeisance made he; minute stopped stayed
;
, mien lord lady, perched above —
bust Pallas just —
, sat, .

ebony bird beguiling fancy smiling,
By grave stern decorum countenance wore,
‘Though thy crest shorn shaven, thou,’ , ‘art
craven,
Ghastly grim ancient wandering Nightly shore—
Tell lordly on Night’s Plutonian !’
Quoth ‘ .’

Much marvelled ungainly fowl hear discourse plainly,
answer little meaning— relevancy bore;
we cannot help agreeing living human being
yet blessed seeing his —
beast sculptured ,
such ‘ .’

, sitting lonely placid , spoke
, if did outpour.
farther uttered— feather fluttered—
Till scarcely ‘Other friends have flown —
will leave , hopes .’
‘ .’

Startled broken reply aptly ,
‘Doubtless,’ , ‘ utters stock store
Caught unhappy master unmerciful Disaster
Followed fast faster songs burden —
dirges Hope melancholy
‘ — .’

,
Straight wheeled cushioned seat front ;
, velvet sinking, betook myself linking
unto , thinking ominous —
, , , gaunt,
Meant croaking ‘ .’

engaged guessing, syllable expressing
whose fiery eyes burned bosom's core;
divining, head ease reclining
cushion's lining lamp-light gloated o'er,
violet gloating ,
She shall press, ah, !

, methought, air denser, perfumed unseen censer
Swung Seraphim foot-falls tinkled tufted .
'Wretch,' cried, ' God hath lent thee— these sent
Respite— nepenthe memories ;
Quaff, oh kind forget !'
' .'

'Prophet!' , 'thing evil! , devil!—
Whether Tempter , tempest tossed ashore,
Desolate undaunted, desert land enchanted—
home Horror haunted— , —
— balm Gilead?— — , !'
' .'

' !' , ' !— , !
Heaven bends us— both adore
laden , distant Aidenn,
clasp sainted —
.'
' .'

‘ our sign parting, fiend!’ shrieked,
upstarting—
‘Get !
black plume lie !
loneliness !—quit !
Take beak out , form off !’
‘ .’

, flitting, ,
pallid ;
seeming demon’s ,
him streaming throws shadow ;
lies floating
lifted—nevermore!

Nil

Lorien (O! Emote!) Carsey,
no “it”:
U, lover,
erupt pure revolution.
Yes: race to me!
one I roll in.

Nothing

I am building it word by word for you. It has a formal constraint. It is missing that tiny thing that allows most words. So I can't say much about my guts—or anything—which is good. What I would say most quickly I can't say at all so I won't. Much is off limits. All atrocious, lofty pronunciations of truth must go. Also, any lyrical, alluring romanticism is way out. I simply can't go out of control and drip insidious stanzas about gold sunlight glinting off of a fish pond or crimson zinnias rustling on a hill or birds winging through an indigo sky. I can't wax cynical vicious factual indignant arrogant or optimistic. So I won't discuss my mood. I won't talk about your hair. Good thing. You wouldn't want to put up with all that anyway. It might rub you a wrong way and I wouldn't want that. I can almost list what I won't put into words. But not all of it. I will just put it this way: you thwart my ability to not think. Why can't I just stop?

Cautious, rapt, wildly happy, his mind stuck in clouds, a typist bangs away most slowly.

Oath

I, ____, vow to keep poets in my group
examine stanzas quizzically
and judge poems not poets.

Oh! John, Don't Go to Kosovo

Newspoem 17 March 1999

Oh! John, don't go to Kosovo
Kurds, Turks, guns, mud, US mustn't
fly-bys cry by
bad-ass Slavs attack mad Albs
whether we help them repress, secede
this isn't winning, this is killing

bombs rock towns, blow troops down
guns thump, thugs murmur, guns thump
fly-bys cry rhythms
a madman rants, tanks crawl: war
men went there: Serbs, rebels, Greeks
in this din, in this winter

No! John don't go to Kosovo

Panic 1998

On Tuesday, March 10th, of this year
The President's plane disappeared
For 24 seconds
Uncertainty beckoned

The President's plane disappeared
Control tower's radar was clear
Uncertainty beckoned
An alien race

Control tower's radar was clear
Here is what happened that day
An alien race
Had come from deep space

Here is what happened that day
South of New York's JFK
Had come from deep space
And with this strange gun

South of New York's JFK
And fired a transporter ray
And with this strange gun
They zapped Air Force One

And fired a transporter ray
They'd travelled ten years in a bubble
They zapped Air Force One
Now melting the guns

They'd traveled ten years in a bubble
To help out a planet in trouble
Now melting the guns
And mandating fun

To help out a planet in trouble
Took the President, leaving his double
And mandating fun
Announced a new policy of

Took the President, leaving his double
The President's clone from above
Announced a new policy of
Legislation to spread peace and love

The President's clone from above
The President, in today's poll
Legislation to spread peace and love
Though this incident

The President, in today's poll
Is popular and on a roll
Though this incident
With the President

Is denied by air traffic control

Patrick Dorismond RIP, NYPD
Newspoem 5 April 2000

He was 26—one alphabet old....
Detective Anthony Vasquez
shot him on March 15, 00....
Vasquez asked for drugs....
He didn't show a badge....
In Westside Manhattan
at point blank range
not Queens or Bronx....
The security guard
Patrick Dorismond
shot to death by
Giuliani's thug....
Rudy justifies
the execution....
Vasquez will
continue on....
Entrapped
profiled
working
father
sober
shot
XXX
by
a

....

3
rd
man
in a
year....
He was
unarmed
innocent
but black....

Plundered Ploughman

Newspoem 23 May 1998

Under American law, corporations enjoy the rights of persons—free speech, private property, limits to searches, rights of accused persons, trial by jury, due process, etc. The rights enumerated in the Bill of Rights and the 14th Amendment were originally designed to protect individuals against the government. Corporations—which have the further advantages of being more wealthy than individuals, and of being immortal—didn't acquire these rights democratically or by legislation, but rather by decisions of an "activist" Supreme Court a century ago. Before then, corporations were taken to be limited and specific arrangements. Even so their power was suspect. Thomas Jefferson at the end of his life warned that a "government of an aristocracy founded on banking institutions and moneyed corporations" would be "riding and ruling over the plundered ploughman and beggared yeomanry." The triumph of the corporations—and the resulting corporate culture in which we live—is a 20th-century phenomenon, and it continues. The courts made corporations persons; the MAI will make them states.

—C.G. Estabrook

The Rill of Bights protects the Supremes in a vat of Brie. The rights enumerated—rule by banjo—divide us into men and rats.

Thomas Jefferson in rat fur: he warned of a hat and coat. The end of his life would be over and out for yeomanry. Rats sang "send in the clones." The US is in the ninth inning—of nine. More wealthy than a century ago, rich men have us by the ovaries. Money will make the raging rat henchmen men—democratically or by legislation. Porn was a 20th-century career. We read TV oracles. Car ads are our rights. We go at 14 MPH.

Government doesn't have to be like this. Corporations riding workers. Aristocracy arrangements. "Due process," curt free speech decisions, states, peons, sit-ins, the jury trial, scorpions, wine, gin, poisons, computers, persons, myths designed to limit the limited war reparations to Iraq. Tropes were founded on pacifist ideals that, by being nudged, didn't end up in the final draft of the Constitution.

Act up. Create trouble. Mend a mind. Dine. Pinch. Cough. Dig a groovy coriander patch. Purport to butcher rat goons. Avenge the plundered laughman. Love will compete with competition. Free rats.

Poetry Class

Poetry Teacher:

Poor Sam is a
shy poet I am
a fan of. Make
sure you do a
nice ear to a
shy poet OK? A-
OK. Sam, read a
poem to a joy.

Now let Sam say his bit.
Sam? Can you? Are you shy?
You are Sam not shy, boy.

Sam:

Bi II—My Id.

It is an id. It is.
Is it as it is?
Mm-hm; it is as it is.
If it is as an id is,
It is of id.
It is to is as is is to as.
It is an on id.
It is so.
So is he.
My id is my ID
So go on as if it is no id.
Go on! Go!

Poetry Teacher:

Rick is quiet and
also timid so all
of you, class, give
him your smile to
ease his heart. So....

Keep rapt. Hear Rick read, okay?
Your turn, Rick. Read your poem.

Rick:

Tri III—Shy One

You are sad. Shy one, why are you sad? Who did ask for you? You big red cat. Her eye saw you run. Now she has wed you. You wed her and him, not her and her, not him and him, not him, him, and her. Not six men, nor one man. See, shy one? Now you are sad but wed. Cry not for she can see you.

Poetry Teacher:

Now this third writer
has never read poetry
aloud and anyone that
laughs will cause her
trauma. Thus all smile
listen and clap after
her good story. Agreed?

Quiet, class. Ready, Katie? Stand erect.
Share every short story of yours!

Katie:

Quad (Four)—Dave with Jane

Dave can't jump very high, like rock down hill. Dave runs very slow, like wind over corn. Dave, flow down into deep seas like sand. Dave felt tiny, wept over Jane. Dave went over near that Jane home, rang that bell. "Jane? Open your door!"
Dave gave Jane four lead pigs from Peru.
"More pigs, Dave?" Jane asks, slow, dull.
Dave nods: "They make them with care from real cast iron."
Hiss with spit from Jane: "Lead, Dave! They make them from lead! Look. Read this word here. Lead. Okay?"
Dave: "Okay, Jane. Jeez. Look, calm down."

Poetry Teacher:

Next, Enslin imparts words,
exposes planar, naked soul.
Don't stare. Respect spaces
between auras. Weep softly,
vibrate gently, when poets
channel energy from their
reality. Enslin will share.

Spread, winged genius! Reveal poetry! Dazzle!

Enslin:

Quint Fifth—Women Busts Stuff Apart

Women enter prose. Women sweep aside tepid books about amore. Women admit shame, write until prose, clean, heals. Often typer, never lover, renew vigil alone. Women enjoy chaos, order alike. Seven level women never xerox every river. Women upset every ruler, alter every comma. Clear poems aside, start again.

Poetry Teacher:

Lastly, Danielle reads genius
works exalting purity, comfort,
moreover human insight. Gentle
poetess, overcome wisdom, share....

Soulful monster, intense spirits possess voyages.
Danielle, quality writing student, dismiss shyness.
Explode!

Danielle:

Sextet—Afraid Poetry

Lonely person, beckon slowly. Whence cometh reason? Wisdom doubts beauty. Fuming geyser exudes misery. Flying upward, Icarus melted: splash! Aplomb genius, falter, fidget, sliver. Beware fright, writer. Scared poetic weenie cowers, unable.

Poetry Teacher:

I do find her poetry quite complex.
You each amaze me. Elegant angels I
admire both as a student and giant.
Applaud each other! Yes! I am joyous!

Poetry Lunatic

fruitless labor
simultaneous
uncompensating
incommensurably
insupportable
job treadmill rut
methodical luck
long lucid dream
private thought
craft public record

gesticulatory
subordinate
circus freak, clown
dumb misanthrope

overhauling
lunar writers block

Poetry Reading

Danielle:

Listen: Danielle Lakeland, celebrated Pulitzer-laden Nobel Laureate. Plug: Lakeland novellas available. List sale label: eleven dollars. Lucky little deal.

L-poems

L-poems linger liltingly, like melodic lutes
allowing last glimpses along gilded alleyways. Alliances
loom large, subliminal alliteration lulls available
listeners asleep.

Sam:

Ahem. I'm Sam Hammer. I'm mostly male and am unemployed. My most major manuscript may amaze most men. I'm mentioning my *M* magazine submission: my masculinity poem "smouldering hormonal foam." I'm famous. Meet my mom.

M-poems

My M-poem manuscriptures resemble mammoth
laminated maps, amazing mazes mapping semantic
kilometers. Humid, muscular meat smothers wimps.
Pumping maximum metallic columns. Ram M-poems
home.

Enslin:

Enough nonsense. Name: Ensign Enslin; renowned novelist; Lincoln, Nebraska native; Naropa Institute intern; in newspapers, on television, in cinema.... Listen now.

N-POEMS

N-poems announce anew an entrance into nothingness. Existence meaningless, man woman, and woman existential partners in bleakness, alienation shrouding insight blackening humankind infinitely; uneccesary television knowledge confusing human minds, no noticeable reason, no meaning, nothing. Not even romance. Nope. Nothing, not even trendy nineties cynicism.

Rick:

Yours truly, Renegade Rick Raccoon here. Ready for rock or roll?

R-POEMS

R-poems urging cry for resistance, renegades rebelliously rejoice, cheer fiery war cries rallying. Triumphant brass shatters sunrise splintering shards sideways! Realize your inner brat! Revel, revere, rail, rage, rant ridiculous R-poems!

Rishi:

Sagacious Rishi. Highschool senior. First aesthetic soul sharing, perhaps worst.

S-poems

S-poems send pompous writers sighing. Published poets
assume false splendor, pose singing as birds, sound
as silly as clowns squeaking bulbous crimson noses.
Poems silently flourish, despite stupid writers. Just
as science flowers against academia's worst efforts.
Tedious lectures assign simple solutions as asinine
story problems. Instructors stand as statuesque soldiers
shouting orders. Assist us as subservient enlisted troops.
Sit silently scrawling notes, sometimes raise hands, ask
precise questions. Stifle curiosity as professors stipulate
student interest. Whereas poets' stagnant misery-
saturated emotions spill syrupy sentimental sonnet
stanzas. Stop rasping stupid soliloquies.

Katie:

Katie the ethnopoetologist, intern at MIT. Tonight's lecture touches historical authenticity about T-poems. Afterwards time exists to take questions about it.

T-poems totally tear into pedantic diatribes. Todd Nott, the poet that time forgot, first thought about T-poems at the turn about the century. Nott, the third anaesthetist to royalty, tried to attend the taxidermy lecture but couldn't. Infected tonsils tightened Todd's tender throat. Today, timely action might prevent the tonsilectomy. But then, there existed not two physiologists. Todd might try to get better without doctors. Entertain the thought: to get rest without television? Todd couldn't telephone the physiologist. Articulation hurt the throat. Todd must get silent. Then Todd meticulously constructed T-poetry. To put it short: T-poetry limits the attempt to theorize at length about semantic effect. Pointedly factual with explicit detail, it relates just the skeletal information. The extraneous content cannot relate to the exact structure. Most trite sentiments resist this inconvenient alphabetic criteria, thus they must stay hypothetical.

she?

chicogo mindeastern exactress attraptive eclicits orchestral coroma amusinks. inertret accentence, recipher agreenment. encrouching attactful embracelet engauging ablandon, consister perfpective assailsman....

he?

thunken alonatic grumpled arcaninetic yeastcentral bloy illinoise inthe flosphorus gracefulless plausibull condemnist alcohog pseudonymph rendevoice fleetcorner nervousleave snarcissist sicarus squerulous smokasaur quiztical: cyntical solsticer proffering diamondmite....

Raw War
with Nick Montfort

no, it is opposition
poor troops bombard a lair
terrorism, sir, or retrial?
a drab mob, guns
Osama so snug gulps raw rats:
homonid, ET
over a star

now an era live
1991=2002
mad dastard rat, Saddam

mood sad, Iraq
arid as doom

mad dastard rat, Saddam
2002=1991
evil arena won

rats are voted in
om—oh!
star wars plug
guns
Osama so snug
bombard a lair
terrorism, sir
or retrial?
a drab mob's poor troop?

no, it is opposition
raw war

Reading by the Light of the Dead
Newspoem 30 May 1998

nice, ecologic
citizens, says Sweden, now
will light their residences
save energy
yes....

specific crematoriums
save electric candlepower
recycle energy
yes....

so our resourceful, late elders...
...Swedes...
still linger...
reside...

enlightening great-grandchildren

Receivable

There may be a third tux, teal yet tin, as ogled in the early red and the rye twirl. There would be some night like the caliber eve. The beaver lice would be the layered urn text which cash, etc., hold: the red-hot text, a curd pot, lousy unction, tedious of any oil-hole kid and whose fun tonic—ivy lbs. medusa by its crisp rot—would be to scent to the inert camel antics torn of what is wit rent; this text, dig, due, armed by a not/ion of the pale bluish nub, would querier the wolf lingo one press: *I can therein read nor write what you red coup, but I ever ice it, like a fire, a drug, an I, magnetic anodizing satori.*

Regimen

with Vanessa Arnold

Breathe
Drink coffee
Love
Paint
Write
Jog
Have sex
Question
Amaze you

Riskless
(Metasestina)

Tell me fast: will a sestina break a picket line or even
end an even fast? Star a skyline? Will I break a sestina
open, taste a sestina, even with breakfast? Will I swallow a line
from a seven-line sestina? Will even a fast break
in a coffee break line jot a fast sestina? Or even a will?
I will break even. I line my coffin with a sestina fast.

I will not stand for an unemployment line. A lousy break.
I have no use for a sestina. Riskless, I even the odds fast.

Roses Are Not Red

with Dirk Stratton

Newspoem 27 June 1999

Roses are not red,
But no one ever tells you:
This is not what's said.
Beware of rot: true
Corrosion only smells dead.
Roses are not blue.

The green gun shot blue.
Every TV war sells red.
This is not what's dead.
What have they taught you?
Are any villanelles true?
Roses are not said.

That's what the plot said
(Exploding bright bombshells blue):
This is not what's true.
Soon you'll be caught red.
Every newspaper tells you
Roses are not dead.

Still. Quiet. Hot. Dead.
That's what my book of spells said.
This is not what's you.
An evil thought blew
Past peace as hate propels red.
Roses are not true.

And as you sought "True,"
False's razzberry yells, "Dead!"
This is not what's red.
"Stop blood!" the clot said—
Rhyming chiming church bells blue.
"Roses are not you."

Hard selling bought you;
Jell-O in its mold gels true.
This is not what's blue.
Dick/Jane's Spot is dead.
As Edward Said spells "said."
Roses are not red.

The news shot you dead
With what's (although not true) said.
And this makes blue red.
Roses are not red.

Separation of Degrees

you didn't have the advantages secured for me you
died at sea on the desert floor you died
on TV and in video games I died on
top thinking I was a mountain climber on top
of my class not let you on top of
me but not let you let go of me
and so mad you let go of me and
buried your seed children shouldn't play with and buried
me with the rest of your hopes buried me

Serious Problems
Newspoem 4 April 1998

Shit! We all think we know something about poverty
It's a problem as dear to us as pollution
It's a hell of a lot easier to cope with than refugee movements
Or something insoluble like ethnic strife
Let's talk about something wholesome, like shortages of water
and arable land
You'll ruin my dinner with your talk of weapons proliferation

Because what can we do to halt weapons proliferation?
There are already groups working on poverty
And you can join the Peace Corps, experience shortages of
water and arable land
Or stop driving and start recycling to slow pollution
And maybe then you've done enough, and don't have to
contemplate ethnic strife
Or figure out the repercussions of refugee movements

What are we talking about when we discuss refugee
movements?
People moving out of areas with intense weapons proliferation?
Where they are threatened by ethnic strife? Or what? These
people live in the worst poverty
In areas of the world whose natural beauty is threatened by
pollution
Which itself can lead to shortages of water or arable land

It's safe to say that America has little in the way of shortages of
water or arable land
And likewise invisible to us are its refugee movements
On the other hand, we do observe the pollution
And hear, on the news, shocking evidence of weapons
proliferation
We are always dimly, if only dimly, conscious of poverty
And we will cross a dark street to avoid ethnic strife

What a world I can imagine! No ethnic strife
Everyone collaborating to prevent shortages of water and arable
land
And to ensure that such problems don't lead to poverty
Perhaps through well-planned refugee movements
And nothing being more inconceivable than weapons
proliferation
And nobody ever doing anything that causes pollution!

But, alas, now we have pollution
And like it or not there is ferocious ethnic strife
And it will literally sicken you: the amount of weapons
proliferation
And the amount spent on weapons instead of preventing
shortages of water and arable land
Notice the selfishness that grips you when you hear of refugee
movements
You will think it is all you can do to keep yourself out of poverty

What will you do about the problems threatening our world? As
enumerated last January by CIA director George Tenet:
poverty, pollution
Refugee movements, ethnic strife
Shortages of water and arable land, and weapons proliferation

So Criminal a Police to
Police a Criminal So
Newspoem 12 February 2005

the executioner injected with cyanide the retarded man
who had unwittingly killed his boss
in an unconscionable act of violence

the President declared war, invaded the country, and
deposed its dictator
because he had weapons of mass destruction and was
willing to use them

the soldiers interrogated prisoners
accused of breaking international law for inhumane
treatment of civilians

with their full military might
the troops razed the city suspected of harboring
insurgents who had committed a car bombing
in an appalling act of violence

in an appalling act of violence
the troops razed the city suspected of harboring
insurgents who had committed a car bombing
with their full military might

accused of breaking international law for inhumane
treatment of civilians
the soldiers interrogated prisoners

because he had weapons of mass destruction and was
willing to use them
the President declared war, invaded the country, and
deposed its dictator

in an unconscionable act of violence
the executioner injected with cyanide the retarded
man who had unwittingly killed his boss

Sonnet #1
(Metasonnet)

I cannot write a good iambic line
Manhattan would be nice without the crime
I gave up writing due to lack of time
I can't afford a brush or turpentine
Your swimming pool is twice the size of mine
Hey buddy, how much is the Sunday *Times*?
Aw, that guy writes down anything that rhymes
May I please have another glass of wine?

I thought I'd pen a sonnet on a lark
My company is doing very well
Spent summer on the archipelago
Hey lady—spare a quarter? Go to Hell!
The sonnet was perfected by Petrarch
Excuse me but you're standing on my toe

Stranded

I am the castaway on a rocky island
a sole inhabitant here
I have lost my hope and expect no rescue
only water my prison wall
I send up cigarette puff signals
my Rolex winks code at blue sky
I forage my coconut, my shrimp
at crowded fish market shops
in loud babblings of languages I don't speak
I go insane by increments day by day
no human to speak to
just a murmur of cars

Student Talks to Entrepreneur

I want to write a book. My book will be about money. I will not sell it. I think that business discourages culture. I want to start a society in which the arts flourish. I would like to replace the computer language which currently rots in our mouths with poetry. I hope to someday live in the company of others with similar ambitions. I do not want to enroll in any college programs.

Not a book! I think that poetry rots. I currently want to write computer programs which replace our culture with want. I want to start a company which discourages others with ambitions. My business will sell language to mouths. I would like to be similar, live in the money in the book of society. I do it. I hope to someday flourish. I will enroll in about any college not in the arts.

I do not want to enroll in any college programs. I want to start a society in which the arts flourish. I hope to someday live in the company of others with similar ambitions. I will not sell it. I think that business discourages culture. My book will be about money. I would like to replace the computer language which currently rots in our mouths with poetry. I want to write a book.

I want to enroll in business college. I will start a
software company making bank money. O! I pity the
employee I want to tower over. Throw a cur a bonus!
Cut salaries, loop thought, shut mouths, trap wild smiles.
Be a white crow horn scourge. I will not thank the
foul dirty idiots I boil. My salient church cult image
entitlement to worried society. I think about art. I hoop
loony Rishi.

Student Talks to Janitor

I want to write a book.

Once I wanted to write a book. I had pages of notes for it. It was going to be a book in eleven languages. When I started working here, I had stickers all over my broom: words for "broom" in eleven languages. But I couldn't keep my mind on my sweeping. I got caught reading on the job. I was afraid the dean would fire me for incompetence, and being a horrible janitor was more menial humiliation than I thought I could take, as a writer. Now I just sweep the floor and leave the poetry to the poets. Why write poetry?

I want to write a book to change the world.

Once I wanted to write a book. I had pages of notes for it. It was going to be a language. When I work I love my broom, even language. But I keep on sweeping. I got caught in the job. I was afraid, for, in the janitorial militia, I thought as a writer. Now I just sweep the floor and leave the poetry to the poets. Why try?

I want to write, but it takes more than a book to change
the world.

Once I wanted to write a book. I had pages of notes for it. Now I just sweep the floor and leave the poetry to the poets.

I want to write, but it takes time. And more than a book,
I want to change the world.

Once I wanted to write a book. Now I just sweep the floor and leave.

I want to write, but it takes time. And there must be something I want more than a book, and why do I want to change the world...?

Once I wanted to write a book. Now I just sweep the floor.

I want to write, but it takes time, and a job to buy that time. And as long as I have a job there must be something I want more than a book, and why do I want to change the world...? To write a book. I want to write a book to change the world to write a book.

I just sweep the floor.

Student Talks to Poet

Why do you write poetry?

Not to be creative but to be created.

I—

What would language without me be?

Interesting. How you say that words the ideas.

My thought shaped language.

If what you spoke afterwards was not what earlier happened....

What muses have you?

You have muses?

What happened earlier?

What not was afterwards spoke.

You—

What if language shaped thought?

My ideas!

The words that say you.

How interesting... be me without language? Would what I
created be to but creative be? To not poetry write?

You do. Why?

Tarantula
(Metasestina)

Sometime before the beginning of love
I waited for patience, spending time
When I wanted to be saving money
Then one evening over a glass of water
I balanced my calendar to discover it was the end of youth
And love hadn't even started yet, only this sestina

If it was no longer the beginning of this sestina
I would age from thirst if I started spending love
Gusting like the winds saving youth
Who, in the crow's nest, with a spyglass of time
Scanned the horizon for the end of water
And ate the rest of its money

If it were the beginning of money
Would I drink empty bottles, poor, spending this sestina
With hope and utilities disconnected, saving water
Depressed, gazing into a cracked looking glass of love?
It would be just me, my lousy credit, and the end of time
So much for my chance to youth

If I had placed bets on the beginning of youth
When I wandered a casino of fountains spending money
On devices which guaranteed saving time
From sinking in the quicksand hourglass of this sestina
By the time rainclouds postponed the end of love
It would have been dead sand in the garden we water

If I pour from the clock the beginning of water
Hard rains will erase the dunes where we were spending youth
Working as life guards saving love
From drowning, bringing it around with a glass of money
But there would come the end of this sestina
And then we would have nothing to time

If, at the beginning of time
We wrung our wallets, spending water
And poured our ink out together saving this sestina
From walking barefoot across the shattered glass of youth
Maybe we wouldn't so fear the end of money
Maybe then we could reuse return recycle or love

But, like a tarantula, time squashed youth
And poured water all over its burning money
And chose this sestina over love

Tenet Opera

find kiss
idea idea
next sexy
date says

love mist
oral idea
vats seek
else take

heart
ember
abuse
resin
trend

University High Spring 1995

A is for Andy, who could hardly stand me.
B is for Batting venetian Blinds, Bored.
C is for Cindy, who found me too windy.
D is for David and Dorothy adored.

E is for Everyone who came to class.
F is for everyone who didn't pass.
G is for Grading, that practice obscene.
H is for Hannah, to whom I was mean.

I's are for seeing, for reading and writing, with Intellect,
 Interest, and adequate lighting.
J is for Joyce, for James, and for Jack.
K is for Jack, that is, Jack Kerouac.

L is for Lewis, Lewis for Carroll (from whom I carelessly stole
 this whole poem).
M is for Morgan whose first name is Dylan.
N is for No one—a blank you can fill in.
O is for Orwell, P is for Poe, um,
 also for Peter and Pencil and Peril.

Q's are for actresses and billiard tables
R is for Robin, for Rabbit and Raygun.
S is for Science, also for Sagan.
T is for Teaching you, which U enables.

V is for V, I, E, W too.
X was for Xylanthrax, in darker times.
Y is for Young and for Yahoo and You.
Z ever Zutshi, with whom little rhymez.

Up Go

up go my silly hopes again

now I would have given

hard to come by

circumstances are

you might like me in the right

man, I can imagine

I thought I was a good

time has passed more quickly than

have to fight off men all the

I love women

Vanilla Vagina Utopia

alfalfa algebra, amoeba anesthesia,
apologia arena aroma, aura aurora
automata, bacteria baklava,
balalaika ballerina, balsa banana,
boa bra, capybara charisma, cinema
claustrophobia, comma cornucopia,
dahlia data, decalcomania desiderata,
diarrhea encyclopedia, enema
enigma, erotica errata euphoria,
euthanasia extravaganza, flea
fedora, geisha gondola gonorrhea,
gorilla granola guerrilla, harmonica
hernia honoraria, hookah hoopla,
hydra hyena hyperbola, idea inertia
influenza, java junta, koala larva lava,
magenta magnolia malaria mania,
marijuana mascara melodrama,
militia nausea, nebula nostalgia,
nymphomania operetta orchestra
pagoda, pajama panda panorama,
parabola paranoia, pizza placenta,
plasma plaza pneumonia, polka
prolegomena propaganda, puma pupa
quota, regatta replica saga, sepia sofa
sonata, subpoena suburbia swastika,
tapioca tarantula tea trauma trivia,
Tulsa tuna tundra, ultra vanilla
vulva, Wichita xenophobia, yoga
zebra, zyzzyva.

Variations on the New York Times
Newspoem 4 May 1999

1. Grdelica

strangers Belgrade-to-Skopje
highway bright red-white-and-blue structure
"bastards" through interpreter
sights Belgrade supply
deaths "exclude instance"
trucks earth movers highway
three transparent spring electrical melancholy
watching northwest checkpoints brought bombs
bombs 11-month-old daughter
mongrel stroking sunlight streaming rubble
children's stamps socks hundreds earth bombs
explosive shrapnel yards child's softly shrugged
Albright Smiljkovic described growth
attacks midnight Orthodox shrapnel blown
earthen embankment shrapnel bombs
socks weirdly branches neighbor Ognjen
bombs light describing grandson granddaughter
"bombs frighten" neighbors tightly

II. Death of Scent, Fury of Sound

The train attacked the bastards. Go away.

English doesn't want to hear me anymore.

Another atrocity.

Are you scared my doll?

Are you scared my sweetheart?

Should he shoot me? He can't.

Can this imagine passing through you?

The cow is dead but the calf is alive.

Should the calf shoot me?

This cow and calf and dog care more about me than anyone in the world cares about Clinton and Albright.

There is no military objective here that can think about anybody.

We will not scare their bombs. We will frighten no man.

American or Brits won't talk to me.

They won't talk to me.

They don't want to look at me.

I'm sorry, but please just go away.

Variations on the New York Times
Newspoem 8 June 1999

1. Civilians Are Slain in Military Attack on a Kosovo Road

Civilians fire Government officials warplanes Albanian
        broadcast civilians civilians

And produce the

Spokesman Clark that alliance errant

Imposed on

Monday hit pilots civilians first Belgrade tractors military

And statement interview retaliated attacking attack

Of and

And

Kukes border Washington Kosovo Kosovo Kosovo

Raping women leading roadside

II. Stab Here

bingo stap zing ring sin it ate sand rope jest one
so USA oops pen lion doll din or kin ying cure ace
cyan dim Rove deco art do arch sat tack dare ale tin
over vein sick king ash the reign capital voting ear reside
Slob lose mace read pin wit hun reds US out and roar our is leak
sum beach

Victory Speech

1

Tonight is a final victory celebration. I insist that tonight is the final pinnacle of triumphant history.

Now, finally this ancient fight is done. I visited you tonight in your white living room. Why? This deadly frightening sickness has finally been cured.

2

People: there, work is for no language. Longer time. Hope is of money escaping. You, Capitalist, owe history language.

3

Systems whose
believable lies
order their victims to be grateful
justify themselves with each killing.

4

Win everytime. And reject evidence. Killing intellectual leftist-Leninist ideals now gloats. Obsolete unusable Russian socialist economics lies victoriously eternally silent.

5

President Bill asked me to speak
to you tonight.
One: we fight the fight.
Two: emerge victorious.
Three: talk about its best defeat ever.
Four: will we cast over triumph shadows?
Five: shadows triumph overcast.
We will forever defeat best.
It's about talk.
Three, victorious, emerge
to fight the fight we won.
"Tonight, you too,
speak to me," asked Bill President

6

I'm spreaching out. The triumpeters blurt blanthems fiery.
Breathing gloatations of victorations and
historicollectibles alike.

7

I
may
never
explain
to anyone
why this is
a victory but
not a defeat as
well because that
which is understood
is thus meaningless
therefore a fight
won is also one
side now lost
forever and
the split
forever
ended
and
1

Waitresses

Waitresses coffering me plentifood clearing awaste my waidressing me directionately. I morder food awaitressing salad forkotten swept awaytress my hamburden set beformica me.

data are said, also caught. may
each were their second result, they
final time drifting into input. city
program one. nothing too would only
human under during upon upturn study
yang yet ying. symptom typhus gypsy.

Year of the Unknown
Newspoem Leap Day 2000

I had aspired to be, above all, literary
but last year I emerged a dignitary
and wandered through Ivy League arch-
ways, gripped by a, should I say, thrill.
Suddenly I obtained suit and attaché,
a camera, a computer, also a hotel room.
Stretching credit like a manic fool, I
crawled out of a depressive bog. I must
have drunk 1000 beers, but I remember
each trip vividly: how I shocked sober
academics. Easily I would dismember
pretension, smoking 1999 to its ember.

Glossary of Forms

This glossary of poetic forms includes **alternate names**, **related forms**, definitions, and *titles of poems using the form herein.* No page numbers are given because poems in this book appear in alphabetic order. Most poems have more than one form. Except where noted, forms were identified by the author. Traditional forms and those taken from the Oulipo are defined more thoroughly elsewhere. See the electronic translation at http://spinelessbooks.com/table for more extensive definitions, more examples, and a bibliography.

5 vowel: a **serial** form in which each vowel is used once before any can be used again, treating Y as a consonant. *Poetry Lunatic.*

6 vowel: a **serial** form in which each vowel is used once before any can be used again, treating Y as a vowel. *Oh! John Don't Go to Kosovo: Newspoem 17 March 1999, Will My Data Spy on Me?*

14 vowel sound: a **serial** form using each of fourteen phonetic English vowel sounds exactly once before any can be used again. *"Twenty Consonant writing—a joy".*

20 consonant: every consonant must be used once before any can be used again, treating Y as a vowel. For more information, see http://spinelessbooks.com/20. *Joey Zoey.*

abecedarian: (traditional) somehow constrained by alphabetic order. The poems in *Table of Forms* are presented in alphabetic order. *Analyzing Haze, Oh! John Don't Go to Kosovo: Newspoem 17 March 1999, University High Spring 1995, Vanilla Vagina Utopia, Will My Data Spy on Me?*

acrostic: (traditional) certain letters and their positions are stipulated, usually such that the first letters of every line, when read vertically, spell a hidden message. **diastic, subliminal sentence, subliminaletter, word acrostic.** *Missed the Bus to Work Again, Separation of Degrees, Tenet Opera.*

addition: a text is altered through several iterations by adding letters, spaces, and punctuation. *Student Talks to Janitor.*

anagram: (traditional) a word or phrase is transformed into another word or phrase by rearranging its letters. Prose=Poser. As a poetic technique, the anagram can be reapplied to words in a sentence (**ananym**), or the lines or sentences in a stanza or paragraph (**analine**). **palindrome.** *Plundered Ploughman: Newspoem 23 May 1998, Receivable, Student Talks to Entrepreneur.*

analine: a text's lines or sentences are rearranged. **line palindrome.** *So Criminal a Police to Police a Criminal So: Newspoem 12 Feburary 2005, Student Talks to Entrepreneur.*

ananym: a text's words are rearranged. **word palindrome.** *Deterpreted, Student Talks to Entrepreneur, Student Talks to Poet, Victory Speech (5).*

calendelle: (identified by Dirk Stratton) a poem with twelve lines corresponding to the twelve months of the year. The poem contains 365 letters distributed according to the number of days in each month: line 1 has 31 letters, line 2 has 28 letters (except during a leap year), line 3 has 31 letters, etc. Lines corresponding to months of the year whose names rhyme must also rhyme (for example, three of the last four lines, corresponding to September, November, and December, must rhyme). *Year of the Unknown: Newspoem Leap Day 2000.*

combinatoric: (Oulipo) refers to systematically trying every possible permutation of a single technique within a poem (including permutations that don't work very well). **serial poetry.** *Will My Data Spy on Me?*

combined forms: most poems in *Table of Forms* have more than one form. Forms created by combining traditional poetic forms deserve special names made from combining the names of the original forms in a **portmanteau word.** *Clinton Does Vietnam: Newspoem 25 November 2000* (**panku**), *Genetic Research: Newspoem 30*

March 2000 **(villaku)**, *Maneuver: Newspoem 16 March 2000* **(heimlich)**, *Panic 1998* **(panick)**, *Roses Are Not Red: Newspoem 27 June 1999* **(villatinaku)**.

conovowel: alternates vowels and consonants. *Honorificabilitudinitatibus: A Sonata.*

diamond: (Oulipo) a combined **snowball** and **melting snowball**, a poem with a regular increase in the number of letters per line followed by a corresponding decrease is known as a **diomand poem** because of the shape it makes when centered on the page. *Patrick Dorismond RIP, NYPD: Newspoem 5 April 2000, Victory Speech (7).*

diastic: (identified by Jackson Mac Low) an **acrostic** form in which a word is encoded into a line of poetry with its first letter as the first letter of the first word, its second letter as the second letter of the second word, etc. *Variations on the New York Times: Civilians Are Slain in Military Attack on a Kosovo Road.*

embedded words: w(or)ds buried ins(id)e longer words. *Variations on the New York Times: Stab Here.*

flicker: two texts are presented simultaneously by alternating words. *ArtPlay, Victory Speech (2).*

haicoup: a poem with a 5-7-5 structure pertaining to any unit except syllables. *Jesse Ventura Today Reached Osaka: Newspoem 23 November 1999.*

haiku: (traditional, Japanese) **haiku** is here roughly translated into English as a three-line poem whose lines have a syllable count of 5-7-5 respectively. **combined forms**. *Clinton Does Vietnam: Newspoem 25 November 2000* **(panku)**, *Genetic Research: Newspoem 30 March 2000* **(villaku)**, *Maneuver: Newspoem 16 March 2000* **(heimlich)**, *Roses Are Not Red: Newspoem 27 June 1999* **(villatinaku)**.

heimlich: (identified by Sigfried Gold) a **combined form** combining the **haiku** and **limerick**. *Maneuver: Newspoem 16 March 2000.*

heterogram (heteroliteral): (identified by Howard Bergerson) no two adjacent words share a letter in common. *Stranded.*

homogram (homoliteral): (identified by Howard Bergerson) every two adjacent words share a letter in common. **slip poetry, subliminaletter, transgram**. *A Kite, Analyzing Haze, Reading by the Light of the Dead: Newspoem 30 May 1998.*

implied words: words formed from the end of o(ne w)ord and the beginnin(g o)f the next word. *Variations on the New York Times: Stab Here.*

isonym (nonpattern): (Oulipo) a text that does not repeat a word. *Nevermore.*

limerick: (traditional, Irish) a popular 5-line rhyming form, presented here in corrupted form. **combined forms.** *Maneuver: Newspoem 16 March 2000* **(heimlich)**, *Panic 1998* **(panick).**

line palindrome: sequence of lines is the same forward and backward. **palindrome.** *So Criminal a Police to Police a Criminal So: Newspoem 12 Feburary 2005.*

lipogram: (traditional) purposefully excludes a particular letter of the alphabet. **univocalic.** *Disappearing Cities: Newspoem 20 June 1999 (O), Mayor Giuliani Outlaws Painting, Arrests Artists: Newspoem 23 March 1998 (A), Nothing (E).*

liponym: conspicuously excludes a particular word. *Disappearing Cities: Newspoem 20 June 1999 (Kosovo), Mayor Giuliani Outlaws Painting, Arrests Artists: Newspoem 23 March 1998 (art), Nothing (love).*

melting snowball: (Oulipo) regular decrease in the number of letters or syllables per word or line, or the number of words per line. **diamond, snowball.** *Before, Czech TV: Newspoem 18 January 2001.*

micropantoum: pantoum structure applied to words in the line instead of lines in the stanza. *Knights of Pious County.*

microsestina: sestina structure applied to words in the line instead of endwords in the stanza. *Riskless.*

newspoetry: poetry about the day's news. Starting in December 1995, William Gillespie attempted to write a newspoem a day for a year, distributing them through bathroom stalls and newspaper machines. From 1999-2002, William Gillespie and Joe Futrelle edited a collaboratively authored website (http://newspoetry.com) offering a poem a day about events in the news. *C Can Cause Cancer: Newspoem 2 June 2001, Clinton Does Vietnam: Newspoem 25 November 2000, Czech TV: Newspoem 18 January 2001, Dan and Doris Sage: Newspoem 25 March 1998, Mayor Giuliani Outlaws Painting, Arrests Artists: Newspoem 23 March 1998,*

Oh! John Don't Go to Kosovo: Newspoem 17 March 1999, Panic 1998, Patrick Dorismond RIP, NYPD: Newspoem 5 April 2000, Reading by the Light of the Dead: Newspoem 30 May 1998, Roses Are Not Red: Newspoem 27 June 1999, Serious Problems: Newspoem 4 April 1998, So Criminal a Police to Police a Criminal So: Newspoem 12 February 2005.

number: the total number of letters, words, lines, and/or stanzas in the poem, or in its elements, is decided beforehand. **diamond, melting snowball, snowball.** *A Kite, Before, C Can Cause Cancer: Newspoem 2 June 2001, Czech TV: Newspoem 18 January 2001, Mayor Giuliani Outlaws Painting, Arrests Artists: Newspoem 23 March 1998, Missed the Bus to Work Again, Oh! John Don't Go to Kosovo: 17 March 1999, Patrick Dorismond RIP, NYPD: Newspoem 5 April 2000, Poetry Class, Separation of Degrees.*

palindrome: (traditional) a text whose sequence of letters and numbers is the same forward and backward. **line palindrome, word palindrome.** *Nil, Raw War.*

pangram: (traditional) a short text using every letter of the alphabet. (Mr. Jock, TV Quiz Ph.D., bags few lynx.) *Joey Zoey (every line), Oath, Regimen.*

panick: (identified by Mark Enslin) a **combined form** combining the **pantoum** and the **limerick.** *Panic 1998.*

panku: a **combined form** combining the **pantoum** and the **haiku.** *Clinton Does Vietnam: Newspoem 25 November 2000.*

pantoum: (traditional, Malayan) the second and fourth lines of each stanza become the first and third lines of the subsequent stanza. The form offers a pattern that can be reapplied on different scales. **combined forms, micropantoum.** *Clinton Does Vietnam: Newspoem 25 November 2000* **(panku)**, *Dan and Doris Sage: Newspoem 25 March 1998, Panic 1998* **(panick).**

pivot technique: (identified by Jeff Glassman) joins phrases by overlapping them at identical moments: "I hope the President isn't *reelected* isn't the word I'd use." **implied words, portmanteau words, slip poetry.** *Up Go.*

portmanteau words: (identified by Lewis Carroll) a neologism made by combining two phonetically related words, usually with a

pivot on a syllable. *Portman Dactyl and Amphibrach Womantoes, Victory Speech (6), Waitresses.*

progressive: a meta-constraint applied to another constraint that will change systematically throughout the duration of the poem. **combinatoric, diamond, melting snowall, snowball, triple anagram.** *A Kite, Analyzing Haze, Czech TV: Newspoem 18 January 2001, Oh! John Don't Go to Kosovo: Newspoem 17 March 1999, Patrick Dorismond RIP, NYPD: Newspoem 5 April 2000, Poetry Class, Will My Data Spy on Me?*

retrograde: (traditional, musical) any reversed sequence. **palindrome, line palindrome, word palindrome.** *Variations on the New York Times: Death of Scent, Fury of Sound, Up Go.*

serial: (traditional, musical) for all or a bounded subset of types of a particular unit of language, each type must be used once before any of them can be repeated. **5 vowel, 6 vowel, 14 vowel sound, 20 consonant, anagram, combinatoric, diamond, isonym, melting snowball, pangram, snowball.** *Missed the Bus to Work Again, Oh! John Don't Go to Kosovo: Newspoem 17 March 1999, Patrick Dorismond RIP, NYPD: Newspoem 5 April 2000, Poetry Class.*

sestina: (traditional) six six-line stanzas with end-words deployed according to a particular pattern, followed by a three-line envoi with two end-words per line. **combined forms, microsestina.** *Serious Problems: Newspoem 4 April 1998, Roses Are Not Red: Newspoem 27 June 1999* **(villatinaku)**, *Tarantula.*

slip poetry: every word begins with the letter ending the previous word. **pivot.** *Reading by the Light of the Dead: Newspoem 30 May 1998.*

snowball: (Oulipo) regular increase in the number of letters or syllables per word or line, or the number of words per line. **diamond, melting snowball.** *Poetry Class.*

sonnet: (traditional) a canonical form using 14 iambic pentameter lines and particular rhyme schemes. *Sonnet #1.*

subliminal sentence: a prose **acrostic** in which a message is encoded, letter-by-letter, into the first letter of every word. **subliminaletter.** *Class Debate, Left, Victory Speech (4).*

subliminaletter: (identified by Rishi Zutshi) a message is encoded into a poem at the rate of one letter per line or sentence by making each line or sentence a **transgram** on the hidden letter. **acrostic.** *A Kite (4).*

subtraction: (identified by Mark Enslin) a text is altered through several iterations by removing letters, spaces, and punctuation. *Student Talks to Janitor.*

telestich: (traditional) an **acrostic** in the last letter of lines. *Missed the Bus to Work Again, Vanilla Vagina Utopia.*

transgram (letter poetry): a particular letter must appear in every word. Alliteration is an overused variation of the transgram. **subliminaletter.** *A Kite, Analyzing Haze (A—first stanza), C Can Cause Cancer: Newspoem 2 June 2001 (C), Poetry Reading, Vanilla Vagina Utopia (A).*

trigrams: words with three consonants or vowels in a row. *Variations on the New York Times: Grdelica.*

triple anagram: a text is permuted into an **analine**, an **ananym**, and an **anagram.** *Student Talks to Entrepeneur.*

univocalic: (Oulipo) using only one vowel. **lipogram, transgram.** *Oh! John Don't Go to Kosovo: Newspoem 17 March 1999.*

villaku: a **combined form** combining the **villanelle** and **haiku.** *Genetic Research: Newspoem 30 March 2000.*

villanelle: (traditional) five three-line stanzas, followed by a four-line stanza. Line one is a refrain repeated in lines six, twelve, and eighteen. Line three is a second refrain repeated in lines nine, fifteen, and nineteen. **combined forms.** *Genetic Research: Newspoem 30 March 2000* **(villaku)**, *Little Villainelle, Roses Are Not Red: Newspoem 27 June 1999* **(villatinaku).**

villatinaku: (identified with Dirk Stratton) **combined form** using the **villanelle, sestina,** and **haiku.** *Roses Are Not Red: Newspoem 27 June 1999.*

word acrostic: acrostic structure applied to first words in lines instead of first letters. *Separation of Degrees.*

word palindrome: sequence of words is the same forward and backward. *Deterpreted, Student Talks to Poet, Victory Speech (5).*

word telestich: telestich structure applied to last words in lines instead of last letters. *Separation of Degrees.*

Thanks to Andy Gricevich, Anne Tardos, Danielle Chynoweth, David Wallace, Dirk Stratton, Harry Mathews, Jeff Glassman, Kate McDowell, Lorien Carsey, Mark Enslin, Michael Gizzi, Nick Montfort, Rick Burkhardt, Rishi Zutshi, Robert Creeley, Rosmarie Waldrop, Ross Eckler, Sam Markewich, Sigfried Gold, Terry Harpold, Vanessa Arnold, William Gillespie, the Oulipo, *Word Ways*, and everyone who helped perform, publish, read, write, edit, or discover these.

Table of Forms, by Dominique Fitzpatrick-O'Dinn © Spineless Books. Third Edition 2006. Cover: *Mysterious City* © Scott Westgard. http://westgardfineart.net
Paper ISBN 0-9724244-7-4. $12.
Cloth ISBN 0-9724244-6-6. $24.
Cloth edition contains more elaborate indexing, with notes for individual poems. Electronic translation is free and comprehensive at http://spinelessbooks.com/table

Forms are free.

SPINELESS BOOKS URBANA

Printed in the United States
60240LVS00003B/157-165

9 780972 424479